Table of Contents

W9-AGI-773

Curriculum Overview

Outcome:	Lesson
• Demonstrate an awareness & appreciation of various aboriginal cultures in Canada.	• Sample Morning Discussion Messages • The First Nations • The Woodland First Nations • The Iroquoian First Nations of Southeastern Ontario • The First Nations of the Plains • The First Nations of the Plateau • The Pacific Coast First Nations • The First Nations of the Mackenzie and Yukon River Basin • A Few Famous People of the First Nations
• Demonstrate an awareness of Aboriginal origins.	• Sample Morning Discussion Messages • The First Nations
• Recognize examples of aboriginal artistic & cultural achievements.	• A Few Famous People of the First Nations
• Demonstrate an awareness of contributions of aboriginal peoples to Canadian society.	• A Few Famous People of the First Nations
• Demonstrate an awareness of the relationship between the environment and Aboriginal lifestyles.	• The First Nations • The Woodland First Nations • The Iroquoian First Nations of Southeastern Ontario • The First Nations of the Plains • The First Nations of the Plateau • The Pacific Coast First Nations • The First Nations of the Mackenzie and Yukon River Basin
• Identify current concerns of Aboriginal peoples	• Sample Morning Discussion Messages • A Few Famous People of the First Nations
• Describe early explorers' perceptions of Aboriginal peoples' way of life.	• The Europeans

Teacher Tips

What I Think I Know / What I Would Like to Know Activity

A great way to engage children in a new theme is to ask them what they think they know about a subject and what they would like to know about a subject. Complete this activity as a whole group brainstorming session, in cooperative small groups or independently. Once children have had a chance to contemplate the theme, combine all information to create a class chart to display in the classroom. Throughout the study, periodically update the children's progress in accomplishing their goal of what they want to know and validate what they think they know.

Morning Messages

Morning Messages provide students with interesting facts about the theme they are studying. They may also be used to arrange teachable moments in the use of punctuation, if the teacher chooses to re-write the messages making "mistakes" for the student to seek and correct. Morning Messages are an excellent way to get the learning going when the students enter in the morning. There are several Morning Messages included with this unit.

Reading Cloze Activities

Cloze activities are not only useful for learning new information, but are great to practise reading skills. The children practise reading each cloze page individually or with a friend and finally with the teacher. Initial the page if reading is satisfactory.

Word List

Word Lists create a theme related vocabulary. Place word lists on chart paper for students' reference during writing activities. Encourage students to add theme related words. In addition, classify the word list into the categories of nouns, or verbs and adjectives.

Did you know scientists believe that there once was a land bridge that connected across the top of North America and Asia? It is thought that early man traveled across this land bridge and migrated down the coast of North America. Eventually the lands separated into the Asian and North American continents we know today. The ancestors of the Aboriginal Peoples are directly linked to these early explorers!

Did you know reserves are lands set aside for the use of Aboriginal Peoples only? A reserve is a piece of land that other people cannot hunt, fish or settle on. Often these reserves were too small for First Nations people to keep their traditional way of life. When reserves were created, the Aboriginal Peoples were no longer allowed to hunt and fish in other areas outside the reserve.

Sample Morning Discussion Messages

Did you know Pow Wows are a way of First Nations to gather together to dance, sing and visit? Pow Wows are a way to preserve the respected heritage of the Aboriginal Peoples. Singers play an important part in the Pow Wow. Without song, there would be no dancing. Dancing has always been an important part of the culture.

Pow Wows are organized by committees that work very hard to bring the people together in friendship and dance. The Grand Entry is a parade of all the people involved in the Pow Wow. The flags are brought in first, followed by the chiefs and other important princesses, elders, organizers and dancers.

Drums play an important part of the ceremony. It is believed the drum connects the people and brings them into balance. The drum is the heartbeat of the earth and the Pow Wow.

Did you know a jingle dress is a beautiful garment worn in a Pow Wow? The jingle dress was made from rolled up snuff can lids that were hung together on a ribbon. The ribbon was sewed to the dress. When the dancer moved, the jingles hit together causing the tinkling of the patter of rain.

Sometime the jingle dress is called a prayer dress. It is said that a shaman's granddaughter was very ill. The shaman's spirit guide advised him to have a jingle dress made and have his granddaughter dance in it.

She was too ill to dance, so tribe members carried her around the dance circle. As time passed and the dance continued around the circle, the girl grew stronger. She finished the dance on her own!

Sample Morning Discussion Messages

Did you know the First Nations had their own type of sauna? The sweat lodge was a small hut with a fire pit inside. Rocks were heated in the fire and water was sprinkled on the rocks to create steam. The sweating of the person within the tent was believed to be cleansing both spiritually and physically.

Once cleansed, the person was ready to communicate with the spirits.

In 1867, the Indian Act defined the things First Nations group could and could not do. It set out rules to control the Aboriginal Peoples. The Indian Act made it against the law for more than 3 or more First Nations people to make demands on civil servants. This meant First Nations could not organize themselves to tell their concerns to the government. Around the same time, the reserve system was put into place, as well as residential schools.

It has taken First Nations people many long years of struggling to get some recognition from the Canadian government. They are still struggling to have the right to their own government.

Sample Morning Discussion Messages

Did you know First Nations People were master storytellers? They passed on the traditions and beliefs of the people through story telling. A good story -teller could remind people about things that they had forgotten or make listeners believe they heard or smelled things that were not there! Storytellers shaped the way people thought. Through songs, legends and stories the First Nations people passed on their history, childrearing practices, and cultural heritage.

Did you know in August 1995 the Canadian government began to talk about letting Aboriginal Peoples self-govern? Self-government means making some laws, making choices on how to spend money on things like education, and making decisions in the best interest of the people.

Finally, after many years the Canadian government is working with First Nations people to make sure Aboriginal Peoples have the same rights as all Canadians.

Did you know scurvy is disease that is caused by the lack of vitamin C in the diet? Lack of vitamin C causes your gums to swell and bleed, weakness and spots on your skin.

When early sailors stayed on ships for long periods of time, they lacked this important vitamin and often were very ill when they landed in Canada. Aboriginal Peoples had learned that the spruce tree buds cured scurvy, and taught early explorers that drinking spruce bud tea made them well again!

Research Reporting Opportunities

Research is a fun way to teach children how to read informational text and express what they have learned in their own words. It is easy to set up a theme related centre. Set up a special table with theme related information materials including, books, tapes, magazines etc.

When introducing the children to the use of non-fiction books as a source for their research writing discuss the different parts usually found in a non- fiction book:

The Title Page: Here you find the book title and the author's name.

The Table of Contents: Here you find the name of each chapter, what page it start on and where you can find specific information.

The Glossary: Here you find the meaning of special words used in the book.

The Index: Here you find the ABC list of specific topics you can find in the book.

Next, discuss with the students the expectations of what a good research project should include:

1. number of interesting facts.
2. the use of proper grammar and punctuation, for example capitals, periods.
3. the size of print so that it is easy to read from far away.
4. the use of good details in colouring and the drawing of pictures.

Assessment Strategies

Unit Test

At the completion of this unit, students participate in a paper/pencil learning inventory test to test their knowledge of concepts covered. The unit test includes true and false, and some written answers.

Constructed Response Learning Logs

Learning logs are an excellent means for students to organize their thoughts and ideas about the concepts presented. Do not emphasize grammar, spelling or syntax. The student responses give the teacher opportunities to plan activities that may review and clarify concepts learned.

Complete learning log entries on a daily basis or intermittently depending on scheduling. Entries should be brief. Time allotted for completion should be less than fifteen minutes.

Learning logs can include the following kinds of entries:
- Direct instructions by the teacher;
- Key ideas;
- Personal reflections;
- Questions that arise;
- Connections discovered;
- Labeled diagrams and pictures;
- Responses to newspaper articles or television programs, videos etc.

Learning logs can take the form of:
- An Aboriginal Journal;
- Entries In Class Journal;
- Reflective Page.

Student Self-Assessment Rubric:
Students use the rubric to evaluate themselves and the work they produce.

Culminating Activity

A summative evaluation of this unit may be done through a class project. The class project is intended to incorporate the expectations of skills of inquiry, design and communication. Children are asked to do the following challenge:

You and your classmates have been asked by the Chiefs of the First Nations Groups to create the ultimate Canadian First Nations Cultural Expo. You need to think about the different territories and other environmental conditions in each of the First Nations groups in order to develop an interesting and concise explanation of your group. Each unit in your class should choose a different First Nations group. Assemble each region to create a class expo.

The following pages include a six-step format that encourages children to use the writing process. In this project, children are asked to create a cultural expo, using a number of suggestions from activity cards provided. Children should be encouraged to add as many details as possible to their project. In addition, a written report should be included. Children may use this report as a reference during an oral presentation.

Other Teacher Tips:

> Create invitations and Invite other classes and parents to share projects and celebrate the learning;
> Decorate the classroom with artwork to support the projects;
> Provide children with sample artifacts or ideas that could be part of the expo.

Culminating Activity: Creation Of A Class Cultural Expo

Step One: (pre-writing) Choosing Your First Nations Group

1. My group of study is:

    ❑   The Woodland First Nations
    ❑   The Iroquois First Nations
    ❑   The Plains First Nations
    ❑   The Plateau First Nations
    ❑   The First Nations of the Pacific Coast
    ❑   The Mackenzie and Yukon River Basins First Nations

2. Gather different types of resources, like CD Roms, books, Internet sites and videos.

3. Use the web planner to organize information.
    These headings are a guide to organizing your work.
    Each heading on your web planner should be a different colour.

    (*E.G. Natural resources could be red, so all the information you find about the resources in your region, will be underlined in red!*)

Culminating Activity: Creation Of A Class Cultural Expo

Step Two: (drafting) Gathering and Organizing Your Information

1. Using one resource at a time, read for information on your topic.

2. Using your information recording sheet, make jot notes in your own words.

3. Using a coloured pencil underline the information according to the colour you chose for your heading on your web.

    (*E.G. If you chose yellow to show all the information you found about climate, it will be underlined in yellow.*)

4. Re-write your information for each heading from the web, so all the information underlined in each colour is together, on a separate page.

Step Three: (revising) Making It Better!

In a small group or with a friend, read your draft for meaning and then add, delete, or change words to make your writing better.

Step Four: (editing) The Final Check

In a small group or with a friend, use this editing checklist to make sure you:
- ☐ used **capitals** at the beginning of sentences and for names and for your titles;
- ☐ have **periods** or questions or exclamation marks at the ends of sentences;
- ☐ used **commas** to separate series of words;
- ☐ **spelled** words correctly.

Culminating Activity: Creation Of A Class Cultural Expo

Step Five: (publishing) Putting It All Together!

1. Discuss with your teacher changes to be made to your work, or if you are ready for the next step.

2. Organize your information on a presentation board.

Think about:
➤ the size of your printing, making sure it is easy to read from far away;
➤ drawing detailed pictures to go with your information;
➤ making a model or diorama, etc. to go with your project.

Step Six: (presenting it) Telling About It

1. Using your presentation board, model or diorama, practice showing and talking about your project:

➤ use your best voice, speaking slowly, and making sure it is loud so everyone can hear;
➤ look at your audience and try not to sway;
➤ introduce your project in an interesting way (Riddle, or Question);
➤ choose the most important things to tell. Use your web planner for ideas;
➤ point to your pictures, model, or diorama, as you present.

Web Planner Page

Use this page to organize your project.
Some headings to choose from: (You should choose at least four)

- ♦ Where is the First Nations Group located in Canada?
- ♦ What is the climate like?
- ♦ Vegetation and wildlife in the region.
- ♦ Special features.
- ♦ Interesting facts.

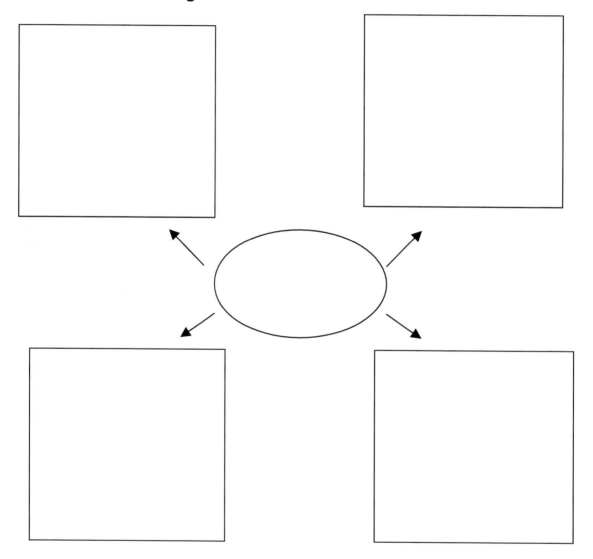

Creation Of A Class Cultural Expo

Resource Title _____

Type of resource: CD Rom   Book   Video   Other

Author of resource: _____

Where I found it: Library   Classroom   Home   Other

This resource was: O.K.   Good   Excellent

Jot Notes:

_____

_____

_____

_____

_____

_____

_____

The First Nations

Did you know that Aboriginal Peoples were the first people to live in Canada? Aboriginal peoples still live all across North America. Each group has its own language, beliefs and laws. In Canada there are six First Nations groups.

When Christopher Columbus landed in the Caribbean in 1492, he thought he had landed in India. He called the Arawak people he met, Indians. This is where the use of the name Indian to describe all Aboriginal peoples over North America began. Today the better names are First Nations or Aboriginal peoples.

There were many differences in **culture**, politics and language, amongst the Aboriginal peoples of North America. The way of life of each group of Aboriginal peoples was linked to the type of land on which they lived. Starting in the east and traveling across Canada towards the west, the present-day groups are: Woodland First Nations, the Iroquois First Nations of Southern Ontario, the Plains First Nations, the Plateau First Nations, the First Nations of the Pacific Coast, and the First Nations of the Mackenzie and Yukon River basins.

Each of these First Nations has **distinctive** and rich traditions. These traditions and cultures are a result of many factors. Some native groups **merged** with others. Some native groups were taken over by larger groups. Other native groups disappeared altogether. These **influences** were sometimes peaceful, while at other times **conflicts** arose. The languages and ways of life of today's First Nations were shaped much the same way as other cultures the world over. Through **evolution** and change, outside influences and necessity to **conform**, the culture we today know as the First Nations of Canada is the product of a complicated process.

There are many differences between the First Nations groups, but there are as well many shared traditions. All First Nations people depended on the land for survival. They were hunters and gatherers. Some added to their hunting skills by becoming farmers. The First Nations used the land as a **source** of medicine as well, and without this in depth knowledge of the earth, First Nations would not have lasted.

First Nations had their own form of government, language and religion. There were **standards** that included political and economic expectations. Whether they were individual, in a clan, tribe or nation, behaviors were expected to conform to the accepted values or laws. The First Nations in Canada were able to live very well using the resources of the natural world around them. The environment in which they lived provided food, clothing and shelter, but the arrival of the Europeans changed their way of life forever!

The First Nations

Find the definitions of the bolded words in the reading.

culture	to join together
distinctive	to do the accepted thing
merged	customs that are followed by a group
influences	disagreements
conflicts	unique characteristics
evolution	growth and progression
conform	power to persuade something or someone
source	ideals or beliefs
standards	place to start or find something

Using information from the reading, and your own ideas tell why the people of the First Nations survived without the Europeans who tried to change their way of life.

_____

_____

_____

_____

_____

_____

The First Nations

G	O	V	E	R	N	M	E	N	T	C	O	T	D	D
A	N	A	D	A	H	A	S	S	I	N	R	L	N	I
T	S	R	I	F	X	F	I	S	T	A	R	A	A	S
S	O	U	T	H	E	R	N	A	D	S	T	N	L	T
N	N	A	A	T	I	I	R	I	O	N	S	G	D	I
A	G	E	R	O	A	I	T	U	P	C	S	U	O	N
T	N	T	G	L	O	I	P	F	R	O	M	A	O	C
U	D	A	P	F	O	Y	R	W	U	A	B	G	W	T
R	G	L	T	N	W	E	U	V	C	S	C	E	M	Y
A	K	P	S	I	L	J	H	K	C	T	F	A	T	B
L	H	A	W	I	O	R	E	S	O	U	R	C	E	S
U	I	O	G	Q	M	N	I	L	K	N	C	D	O	P
B	W	I	Z	D	Z	M	S	P	A	C	I	F	I	C
T	O	A	Z	I	H	R	E	V	I	R	P	U	Y	V
N	A	S	E	U	N	G	L	R	Y	A	B	L	E	V

COAST

PACIFIC

YUKON

MACKENZIE

RESOURCES

ONTARIO

WOODLAND

GOVERNMENT

RELIGION

DISTINCT

NATURAL

FIRST

PLATEAU

NATIONS

SOUTHERN

LANGUAGE

PLAINS

TRADITIONS

RIVER

The Woodland First Nations

Did you know a tribe is a big group of individual First Nations who share a common language and culture? The Woodland First Nations consisted of several tribes. The Woodland First Nations spoke languages belonging to the Algonquian family.

The Beothuk lived in Newfoundland, but are now extinct. The Mi'kmaq lived in Nova Scotia and northeastern New Brunswick, Gaspe in Quebec, and Prince Edward Island. The Malecite occupied Southwestern New Brunswick and part of Quebec. The Montagnais lived along the north shore of the St. Lawrence River in Quebec and the Naskapi lived in Labrador. Along the shores of Lake Huron and Lake Superior to the edge of the Prairies from Georgian Bay, the Ojibway were found. The Odawa lived on Manitolin Island in northern Lake Huron and the Algonquin lived in the Ottawa Valley. Along side the Ojibway were the Cree, who lived on the southern border of Hudson Bay to lake Mistassini, all the way west to the Prairies.

The Woodland tribes had their own territory for hunting and fishing. They were independent of each other. The Woodland First Nations were hunters and trappers. They had excellent knowledge of the seasonal movements of the animals, birds and fish they hunted. They were familiar with the animal habitats and followed their prey to different hunting grounds as the need arose. The native hunters and trappers did not waste any part of their catch. They dried fish and meat they caught along with berries collected, and set it aside for difficult times. Some groups faced starvation as the concentration of game varied from one region to another.

Portable transportation and housing was essential for the Woodland tribes, as their survival depended upon the ability to move with the seasons. They made portable and lightweight homes and methods of transportation.

Stitching sheets of bark together with white spruce roots created the birch bark canoe. The spruce roots were collected in mossy areas under the spruce trees, baked in a fire to make the outer skin crisp and drawn though a notched board to remove the outer skin, exposing the  pliable young root. A coating of heated spruce gum and grease created a waterproofing for the canoe seams. The canoe was lightweight, streamlined, tough, and easy to steer, whether it was being used to collect wild rice, or carrying a hunting party. Made from materials from the forest, it was easy to repair if needed.

Snowshoes were used during the winter months. These large woven, racket-like shoes were used to cross the snowy terrain. Toboggans were used to transport belongings when the rivers froze. Woodland First Nations babies were carried in a moss-lined bag that mothers strapped to wooden cradles so that the babies stood on a little shelf. Tumplines were large sling-like straps that were placed over the backpackers' forehead while the other ends cradled the pack.

The Woodland First Nations

The homes of the Woodland tribes were easily erected and portable. Wigwams were made from a frame of wooden poles and covered with the materials at hand. These materials included woven mats, bark, or animal skins. To ensure ventilation, a hole was cut in the centre of the roof. Conical wigwams were most preferred, but the Ojibway and Cree sometimes used dome-shaped wigwams.

Possessions were stored around the edges of the wigwam, under the supporting poles. The centre of the wigwam was scattered with fir boughs to keep the occupants off the cool, damp ground. The boughs were often covered with fur or rush mats. In the winter, some tribes hollowed out the ground under the wigwam, so the structure was below the frost line. The wigwam could be transported easily by taking the outside covering along on the journey. The wooden poles were easy to find at the next camp.

Birch bark was an important item for the Woodland Nations. It was easy to find, waterproof, and lightweight. Food was boiled in bark containers by dropping heated stones into the water-filled containers. Boxes, baskets and eating utensils were fashioned from birch bark. Women of the tribes often decorated the articles by making exact bites and creating artistic designs. Birch bark could be used to draw maps or write messages upon. A rolled birch bark cone served as a horn by which moose could be lured into an ambush!

Winter was often a time of difficulty, but the Woodland hunters developed methods to overcome the deep snows and harsh climates. Hunters could move quickly on snowshoes, developed for crossing deep snow. Swift hunters on snowshoes easily tracked and overtook animals such as moose or deer stuck in belly-deep snow.

Hunters used bows and arrows, spears, snares and traps to capture their prey, but the most popular method of hunting was stalking. The hunter would carefully track and capture the animal. Sometimes fences were built along paths of moose or deer. Snares were placed in the gaps in the fence, forcing the animals to pass into the snare on the trail. Traps such as the log fall were often used. A log was set to fall when an animal took the bait in the trap. The falling log broke the animal's back, killing it instantly. Snares were made from rawhide or sinew, and caught an animal by its leg or neck. Most Woodland tribes were adept fishermen. They built net-like structures called weirs and placed them across streams to trap fish. The Cree did not fish.

The Woodland First Nations wore clothing made from caribou, moose and deer hide. Men wore tunics, leggings, moccasins and loincloths, while women dressed in much the same way, with the tunics lengthened to the ankle or knees. Fur bearing animals such as the beaver, rabbit and muskrat were used for winter dress. Robes,  mittens and caps were necessary to ward off the cold weather. Pelts were woven together for extra warmth. The Ojibway decorated their clothing with dyes in red, yellow and blue from the summer flowers. Porcupine quill and moose hair embroidery were used to decorate moccasins and gloves.

The Woodland First Nations

Hides were preserved by smoking the skins after removing the fat and soaking it. Hides were stretched and worked with a stone knife. A pointed tool called a bodkin was used to drill holes in the hide. Clothing was joined together with sinew. Sinew comes form the back legs of caribou or moose. A long leather cord called babiche was often used in snowshoes, nets and fastening belongings to canoes or toboggans.

The Woodland First Nations had a great respect for the animals they hunted, and many of their ceremonies and beliefs were connected to this respect. Hunters might carry charms such as beaks, claws or skulls to strengthen their relationships with the animals they hunted. Skulls of bear or beaver were cleaned and placed on poles high above where other animals could not bring shame on them, by eating or carrying them off. Hunters would sing or talk to their prey explaining to it that it's killing was necessary to provide the family with food and clothing.

In his youth, a young man would go on a vision quest. This quest was a search for the spiritual guardian that would aid in his hunting and general well being. Dreams and visions were paid close attention to, for it was believed they told of the future, and could determine good or bad luck.

The shaman was skilled at recognizing and using herbal remedies. He was able to treat the illnesses of his tribe, and often along with the women would place a tube on the affected part of the body and draw out the illness-causing article by sucking on the tube! The Grand Medicine Society of the Ojibway had long periods of training for their members. They participated in a cleansing ceremony to prepare them for the tasks of learning to diagnose illnesses, prescribe herbs and cure the sick. The teaching to become a Medewiwin, as they were known, took many years, and had four levels of organization.

The drum played an important part in the Woodland First Nations ceremonies. Singing, drumming and the use of tobacco were believed to have built the spirit that lived in every human being. This spirit was known as Manitou.

Brainwork: Find five interesting words from the story and define them on a separate piece of paper.

The Woodland First Nations

Fill in the chart below:

Principal Tribes:	
Transportation:	
Housing:	
Uses of Bark:	
Hunting:	
Clothing:	
Ceremonies and Beliefs:	

The Woodland First Nations

Z	C	M	X	V	N	N	R	J	Q	B	D	N	G	O
U	A	A	D	T	V	I	D	E	D	A	Y	A	A	K
Y	N	W	X	H	H	U	K	R	E	Y	M	S	A	K
D	O	G	L	F	C	Q	S	P	A	R	T	K	J	X
N	E	I	M	Z	V	N	N	D	X	U	C	A	I	E
S	Q	W	D	G	U	O	B	I	R	A	C	P	T	M
T	H	S	I	A	N	G	A	T	N	O	M	I	A	S
O	P	T	I	V	B	L	S	B	J	J	C	M	C	K
F	E	O	O	I	N	A	N	I	E	E	O	I	V	R
Y	Z	Y	R	L	J	S	B	E	L	O	N	P	J	A
U	B	C	Y	O	C	W	H	A	L	U	T	P	Y	B
Y	H	B	K	X	A	N	M	A	T	Y	M	H	P	U
A	L	G	O	Y	R	R	I	P	M	U	A	I	U	A
W	O	O	D	L	A	N	D	O	R	A	U	U	Y	K
S	N	A	R	E	S	N	M	D	L	N	N	U	F	Z

ALGONQUIN	BIRCH	CREE
MALECITE	NASKAPI	SNARES
WIGWAM	BARK	CANOE
DRUM	MIKMAQ	OJIBWAY
TRAPS	WOODLAND	BEOTHUK
CARIBOU	LOINCLOTHS	MONTAGNAIS
SHAMAN	TUNICS	

The Woodland First Nations

Use the word box to find the missing word in the paragraph.

The Woodland tribes had their own _____ for hunting and fishing. They were _____ of each other.   The Woodland First Nations were hunters and _____. They had_____ knowledge of the _____ movements of the animals, birds and fish they hunted. They were familiar with the animal _____ and followed their_____ to different _____grounds   as   the need_____.

Word Box

territory	arose
excellent	prey
habitats	hunting
independent	seasonal
trappers	

The Woodland First Nations

Using information from the story, answer the following questions.

1. What is a tribe?

_____

_____

_____

2. Which of the Woodland First Nations is now extinct?

_____

_____

_____

3. What did the Woodland First Nations need to know in order to survive?

_____

_____

_____

4. Why was portable housing important for the Woodland First Nations?

_____

_____

_____

5. How did the Woodland First Nations make their canoes?

_____

_____

_____

6. How did the Woodland First Nations hunters overcome the hardships of winter?

_____

_____

_____

The Woodland First Nations

7. What sort of clothing did the Woodland First Nations wear?

_____

_____

_____

8. Using information from the story and your own ideas, explain a tradition of the Woodland First Nations.

_____

_____

_____

_____

_____

_____

_____

_____

_____

_____

_____

_____

_____

_____

The Iroquoian First Nations of Southeastern Ontario

Did you know there were nine principal Iroquoian tribes? They all spoke languages that came from the Iroquoian family. These tribes were the Huron who lived between lake Simcoe and Georgian Bay; the Tobacco Nation (Petun was another name used) to the south and west of the Huron; the Neutral who lived on the Niagara Peninsula; the Erie tribe who lived on the edges of Lake Erie; and in the area south of lake Ontario to the upper St. Lawrence River were the five tribes of the Iroquois confederacy: the Mohawk; the Oneida; the Onondaga; the Cayuga; and the Seneca.

The Iroquoian tribes were known as a farming group. They planted and harvested crops and lived in **stable** communities. The crops the Iroquois raised were known as the three sisters. They were corn, squash and beans. The beans were planted in the same place as the corn. When the beans grew, they were supported by the tall, strong corn stalks. The squash plants grew between the rows of corn. The large leaves of the squash plants helped to keep the weeds from growing. Huron tribes had dancers dressed in costumes representing the three sisters and they danced to give thanks to the fertility of the earth and the **abundance** of the crops.

The men cleared the land and the women tended the crops. Moose antlers and deer shoulder blades were formed into hoes, which were used to pile the soil into large mounds. Digging sticks were used to make holes in the mounds, and corn seeds were dropped into the holes. When the corn and beans were harvested, they were stored in bark chests inside the houses. Squash was kept in an underground storage chest lined with bark.

The Iroquoian tribes did not have to move as often as the Woodland Natives, because they did not have to search for food. They grew much of what they needed. The village sites that were chosen had to meet certain **specifications**. Good drinking water, good farmable land and a forested area made for a perfect location. The forest provided the needed wood for fire, building homes and shelter from attacking enemies.

The building of a village was not easy. The long house was the main dwelling of the Iroquois. The household usually included a powerful woman, her husband, her unmarried sons and her daughters and their children. Once the sons married, they would move in with the wife's family.

A village of 36 long houses would have about 1,000 people living in it. Long houses were built by lining up a series of parallel poles and bending them into an upside down "U" shape to form a roof. The roof was then covered with bark. Smoke holes were made in the roof and could be widened or narrowed depending on the time of year.

The Iroquoian First Nations of Southeastern Ontario

Each long house was about 10 metres wide, 10 metres tall, and 25 metres long. Families on opposite sides shared **hearths** running down the centre of the long house. Platforms on which the family slept were positioned along the wall above the ground to keep from getting damp, yet low enough to keep out of the rising smoke from the hearths. (See diagram) Wisely the Iroquois built their long houses far enough apart from each other to keep fire from spreading should one break out in the camp. Not having to move gave the tribes stability. Stability gave the tribes time to develop activities for enjoyment and a form of **complex** government.

The Huron government protected the rights of the individual. The clans were able to marry outside their group and they traced their family lines through the female members. Each clan connected with a **totem** animal such as a bear, beaver, wolf or deer. In this way they were easily identified.

The Huron government consisted of a village council, tribal council and the **confederacy** council. The confederacy met once a year, and decisions about the tribes were made when an agreement was reached. Many of these discussions would go late into the night, until the right decisions were made.

Each clan in the Huron tribe had two chiefs. One chief was the war chief, and the other chief was the civil chief. The civil chief played an important role in the clan. He was usually chosen because he was able to perform as a warrior and was smart, generous and able to speak and defend his position well. In other words, he was the political spokes person for the tribe.

The Iroquois had a similar form of government, but there had been a time when the Iroquois fought among each other. They had **raiding** parties in spring and fall, when they went from village to village explaining their war plans and encouraging youth of the tribe to join them. Capturing prisoners made the warrior's reputation bigger.

Tradition has told that a **prophet** named Dekanawideh declared the Great Peace. From his work the council of the chiefs of the five tribes was formed. It is believed that the Iroquois League was formed in the 15th century. The members of the Iroquois League had to be of "one heart, one mind, and one law."

Whenever there was a **dispute** between the tribes, the league met and only a **unanimous** decision could solve the problems. If one of the leagues chiefs died, it was the tribe's oldest woman (the clan mother) who chose a new chief, in **consultation** with the other women members of the tribe.

The Iroquoian First Nations of Southeastern Ontario

The jobs of the men and women of the Iroquoian tribes were well defined. Women of the tribe took care of the crops, gathered the firewood, prepared the skins to make clothing, ground the corn and cooked the meals. They made baskets, mats and pottery. The men of the tribe made the long houses, hunted, fished and made the weapons. They also made the **modes** of transportation such as birch bark canoes.

The Huron believed that everything had a soul. Whether it was something they had made, or the seasons, or other natural events. Young Huron went on "vision quests" looking for the guardian spirit who would tell them their **chant** they would use in times of danger.

The curing masks of the Huron and Iroquois were thought to have a spiritual force that held special curing powers for the sick. The ocata shaman diagnosed and treated illnesses and the aretsan shaman got rid of witches or their spells.

Winter in the Iroquoian tribes was a time for festivals and celebrations. Once a year the Ononharioa or winter festival was said to cure the soul. During the three days of the festival, houses were broken into and the furniture was destroyed. Sick people in the village went through the remains and if they found the things they had seen in their dreams, it was believed their troubles were cured!

The festivals of planting and crop growing were held 6-8 times per season, and occurred during the planting and harvesting of corn. The creator was asked for gardening success and tobacco was burned to assure it.

The Longhouse Diagram:

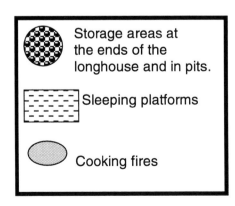

Storage areas at the ends of the longhouse and in pits.

Sleeping platforms

Cooking fires

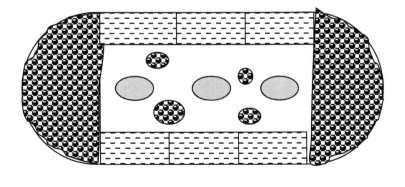

The Iroquoian First Nations of Southeastern Ontario

Fill in the chart below:

Principal Tribes:	
Transportation:	
Housing:	
Uses of Bark:	
Hunting:	
Clothing:	
Ceremonies and Beliefs:	

The Iroquoian First Nations of Southeastern Ontario

Find the definitions of the bolded words in the story.

stable	special conditions or requirements
abundance	looting or rummaging through things
specifications	someone who forecasts or predicts something
hearths	lots of something
complex	an argument
totem	complicated
confederacy	steady or unchanging
raiding	fireplace
prophet	an association or grouping
dispute	good luck charm
unanimous	discussions or talks
consultation	style or type of
modes	repetitive song
chant	everyone agrees

The Iroquoian First Nations of Southeastern Ontario

T	T	V	G	N	B	B	C	A	N	O	E	W	B	B
H	C	O	R	N	E	I	D	X	X	H	Y	I	C	E
S	S	O	B	A	I	I	R	J	K	T	S	G	B	A
T	C	A	V	A	E	G	S	C	Y	O	M	W	Q	N
R	K	E	U	N	C	I	G	D	H	L	S	A	K	S
I	R	T	O	Q	O	C	Q	E	T	C	B	M	W	N
H	K	O	L	U	S	N	O	Y	L	N	S	I	A	N
S	G	E	Q	N	A	M	A	H	S	I	K	I	H	E
O	N	O	N	D	A	G	A	O	S	O	R	E	O	U
S	R	E	C	D	T	O	V	T	I	L	Z	N	M	T
I	E	K	I	H	S	H	E	E	S	U	O	H	V	R
R	D	N	R	J	P	R	M	V	W	R	Q	R	Y	A
A	P	E	E	A	S	C	A	Y	U	G	A	O	Y	L
E	E	H	P	C	B	H	P	H	L	O	N	G	R	R
B	T	D	D	U	A	G	N	I	M	R	A	F	H	I

BARK	BEANS	BEAR
BEAVER	BIRCH	CANOE
CAYUGA	CORN	FARMING
SENECA	HURON	IROQUIOAN
IROQUOIS	LEGGING	LOINCLOTH
ONEIDA	MOHAWK	NEUTRAL
SHAMAN	WIGWAM	SHIRTS
	ONONDAGA	TOBACCO

The Iroquoian First Nations of Southeastern Ontario

Using information from the story and your own ideas tell how the Iroquois First Nations of Southern Ontario and the Woodland First Nations were the same and how were they different. Give examples.

_____

_____

_____

_____

_____

_____

_____

_____

_____

_____

_____

_____

_____

_____

_____

_____

_____

_____

_____

_____

The Iroquoian First Nations of Southeastern Ontario

Use the word box to find the missing word in the paragraph.

The men _____the land and the

women_____ the crops. Moose

antlers and deer _____blades were

formed into, _____ which were used

to pile the soil into large_____.

_____sticks were used to make

holes in the mounds, and corn seeds were dropped into

the holes. When the corn and beans were,

_____they were stored in bark

_____inside the houses.

_____was kept in an

_____storage chest lined with bark.

Word Box

shoulder	cleared
tended	digging
harvested	hoes
chests	squash
mounds	underground

The First Nations of the Plains

Did you know pemmican could be eaten, even after several years? Pemmican was a mixture of dried and powdered meat, melted fat and berries. Women of the First Plains Nations made pemmican and sewed it into skin bags. This high protein food made a good meal to a warrior or hunter and the berries provided vitamin C, important in preventing the disease, scurvy.

There were eight tribes of the First Nations of the Plains. They were the Blackfoot, Blood, Peigan, Gros Ventre, Plains Cree, Assiniboine, Sioux and Sarcee. The Blackfoot, Blood, Peigan, Gros Ventre, and Plains Cree spoke the Algonquian language. The Assiniboine, and Sioux spoke the Siouan language, while the Sarcee spoke the Athapaskan language.

East of the Rockies where Edmonton and Calgary, Alberta are now found today, was the territory of the Blackfoot or Siksika. The Blackfoot, the Blood and the Peigan formed a union that was very powerful. The Blood lived southwest of the Blackfoot in the foothills of the Rockies, while the Peigan lived in the area that we now know as Lethbridge and Medicine Hat, Alberta. The Gros Ventre lived east of the Peigan and the Plains Cree occupied the territory south of the Churchill River, across the northern plains and to the eastern edge of the Blackfoot territory. The Assiniboine territory was south of the Plains Cree to Blackfoot country. The Sarcee occupied the upper part of the Athabasca River. The Sioux (also known as the Dakota) were scattered over what is now Manitoba and Saskatchewan.

The Plains tribes were made of individual groups. Each group had a chief and several councilors. In the summer the groups pitched their teepees in a circle and held council. At this time, they selected a tribal chief or honoured a chief whose power was worthy. Military people of the Plains tribes performed many duties. They policed life in and out of camp, and organized defenses against other warring tribes.

The First Nations of the Plains were a wandering people, following the migration of the buffalo. Dogs were the first means of transporting supplies, before the horse became part of the Plains culture in the 1700's. Travois were two long poles fastened together on a webbed frame for holding articles. These poles were attached to the dogs. Large dogs were known to transport as much as 35 kilograms, and each family owned many dogs.

The Nations of the Plains needed mobile dwellings, as they followed the buffalo. Teepees were the primary dwelling. A foundation of poles in a tripod was firmly planted in the ground. A covering of buffalo skins stitched together was placed over the poles and fastened Poles made from pine trees were transported along with the buffalo skins to cover them. Since trees were not readily available on the Prairies, good strong poles were valued.

The First Nations of the Plains

The teepee was not a simple cone, but was longer along the back, tipping the teepee slightly forward. This allowed for better ventilation and a larger space at the rear of the structure. This shape was also easier to brace against winds that blew across the prairies. The head of the family took the place opposite the door opening, as this was the place of honour. Fur was used for bedding and bags of food were hung from the poles of the teepee.

It was the job of the women of the tribe to care for and put up the teepee. They butchered the meat, drying some to preserve it, and processed the skins to make clothing, and other leather goods.

The buffalo was an important source of food for the Plains First Nation. Freshly killed, the buffalo meat could be boiled in leather bags, making a healthy soup, or dried to make jerky. Jerky was meat from the buffalo that was dried in the sun. It could be keep for long periods of time, stored in leather bags made from the buffalo skin.

 Pemmican was another food that could remain edible for many years. The dried meat was pounded into a powder and mixed with melted fat. It was sewn into leather bags and used by warriors and travelers as a good source of protein. Other leather bags contained "medicine bundles" or good luck charms. When exposed to light the owner would have to sing a special song. These bundles gave the owners wealth and good luck.

Hunting the buffalo was an art that the Plains First Nations peoples perfected. They would arrange bushes, branches and stones along the migration paths of the buffalo, funneling them into an area where they could be easily killed. Bows and Arrows made from ash or willow were the main weapon.

The buffalo jump was a hunting method that made use of the land. Hunters would find an area where the flat plain dropped off into a cliff. They would chase the buffalo over the cliff, stampeding them to their death. This method produced large quantities of meat in one hunt.

The buffalo was not only a source of meat for the Plains First Nation. Every part of the animal was put to good use. Hooves were boiled to make glue. Horns were used for cups and spoons. Sinew from the back of the legs was used to sew and wherever a cord or string was needed. The long hair of the buffalo was braided to make halters for horses and dried buffalo dung made good fuel in areas where wood was scarce. Skin was tanned to make a variety of necessary objects.

The First Nations of the Plains

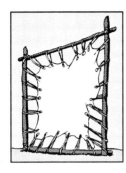

The process of tanning hide was a long and difficult one. The Plains First Nations women worked hard to make the buffalo skin soft and pliable. First they would stretch the skins by pulling it between stakes they pounded into the ground. Next they would scrape the meat and fat off the skin. They then flipped the skin and scraped all the hair off of the other side, until the skin was clean. It was then left to dry, stiff and hard.

To make the skin soft, it was rubbed with animal brains, liver and fat. Sometimes this mixture was worked into the skin using a small smooth stone. The skin was then allowed to dry once more in the sun. Once dry, it was soaked in water and rolled into a ball to cure. After curing, the skin was again stretched and scraped. Finally the skins were rubbed and manipulated until the skin was soft and ready to make into clothing. To cure a buffalo skin, it took the Plains First Nations women about one week.

The clothing made from the buffalo skin usually consisted of breechcloths held up by a belt for men, and shirts that reached below the knees for women. The men also wore long leggings tied with leather thongs. In cooler weather the men wore skin shirts and moccasins. Women wore leggings tied just above the knee.

Headdresses of the Plains First Nations varied. The important Sioux leaders wore full feather headdresses. Other tribes had different headdresses. The Blackfoot wore winter skins of the weasel, making the headdress an impressive white fur. Sometimes the headdresses included the horns of the buffalo, or white eagle feathers. Eagle feathers with the black tips were worn in the hair to mark acts of bravery.

Major warring expeditions between the tribes of the Plains First Nations were usually to find new territory or protect the territory they had. Warfare was well coordinated with surprise attacks, smoke signals and warriors circling the enemy and shooting while tightening the circle. Bows and arrows were the weapons used and shields made from the  tough hide of an buffalo and decorated with feathers were a source of protection.

Along with the warring societies of the Plains First Nations, there were dancing societies. Dances demonstrated the hunting and warfare tactics of the tribe. The dances were usually performed at the summer gatherings.

The Blackfoot Sun Dance was one of the most spectacular dances. The Sun Dance lodge was built before the ceremony, and only a few of the chosen men would dance, fast and pray. In this time-honoured ceremony, self-torture was the end of the dance. Often skewers were forced through the backs of the dancers!

The First Nations of the Plains

Fill in the chart below:

Principal Tribes:	
Transportation:	
Housing:	
Uses of Buffalo:	
Hunting:	
Clothing:	
Ceremonies and Beliefs:	

The First Nations of the Plains

V	E	L	H	Y	V	O	A	F	S	H	U	H	C	Z
D	Q	N	T	E	L	E	E	G	O	L	T	T	I	Z
S	O	N	I	A	A	A	N	R	H	O	S	O	D	Z
D	K	O	F	O	T	D	S	T	O	V	A	L	A	S
V	A	F	L	H	B	E	D	F	R	Q	R	C	M	P
S	U	N	E	B	S	I	K	R	G	E	C	H	O	E
B	U	R	C	K	V	C	N	B	E	C	E	C	N	M
L	S	R	B	E	A	X	Y	I	P	S	E	E	H	M
T	E	A	G	L	E	U	W	R	S	J	S	E	S	I
E	T	C	B	X	I	O	H	U	A	S	K	R	Q	C
A	L	G	O	N	K	I	A	N	I	T	A	B	S	A
E	Z	R	N	I	K	S	K	C	U	B	I	E	Z	N
I	H	O	Q	D	P	E	I	G	A	N	D	L	O	N
N	U	S	J	A	Y	L	L	Q	Z	I	A	Y	I	M
E	E	P	E	E	T	U	B	S	H	W	U	R	H	M

ALGONKIAN   ASSINIBOINE   BLACKFOOT
BLOOD   BREECHCLOTH   BUCKSKIN
BUFFALO   CREE   DANCE
EAGLE   FEATHERS   HORSES
HEADDRESS   HIDES   PEIGAN
MILITARY   NOMADIC   SIOUX
PEMMICAN   SARCEE   TEEPEE
SUN

The First Nations of the Plains

Using information from the story, answer the following questions.

1. Name the eight tribes of the First Nations of the Plains.

_____

_____

_____

2. What is pemmican?

_____

_____

_____

3. What was the job of the military of the First Nations of the Plains?

_____

_____

_____

4. What was the purpose of the travois?

_____

_____

_____

5. Why did the First Nations of the Plains need portable teepees?

_____

_____

_____

6. How was buffalo important to the First Nations of the Plains?

_____

_____

_____

7. Describe two methods of hunting.

_____

_____

_____

The First Nations of the Plains

Using your own words and information from the story, explain the process of tanning hides and making clothing.

_____

_____

_____

_____

_____

_____

_____

_____

_____

_____

_____

_____

_____

_____

_____

_____

_____

_____

The First Nations of the Plateau

Did you know there were six principal tribes of the First Nations of the Plateau? The Interior Salisha was the biggest, made up of five groups belonging to the Salishan language. In the Lillooet River Valley lived the Lillooet tribe. The Thompson First Nations occupied the Fraser River Valley from Yale to Lillooet, and the most northerly and largest group occupying the Fraser River Valley from Lillooet to Alexandria and east to the Rocky Mountains was the Shuswap. The Okanogan River Valley was the territory of the Okanogan. The Lake First Nation also lived in this area, around the Arrow Lakes and the upper Columbia River. The Kootenay tribe migrated to the southeastern corner of British Columbia after being driven over the mountains by the Blackfoot in the 1750's.

The Plains First Nations lived in a diverse and sometimes difficult environment. The valley between the Rocky Mountains and the coastal ranges had many different regions. The south end of the area was a semi-desert, with sagebrush, rattlesnakes and cactus, while the north end was forested and abundant with wildlife such as moose and deer. Between these two expanses was an area of rushing rivers and waterfalls. Salmon ran plentiful in the spring in these waters.

Their neighbours of the Pacific Coast influenced the First Nations of the Plateau. They had close trading ties with the Tribes of the Pacific Coast. The Pacific Tribes had a social organization of nobles, commoners and slaves. The Pacific Tribes believed in supernatural clan ancestors, which the Interior Salish groups adopted. Winter dances where participants wore animal masks also came from the influence of the Pacific Coast peoples. Only the Interior Salish did not adopt the social system.

The salmon migration was a most important time in the First Nations of the Plateau. In the summer, the fish swam upstream to spawn in the headwaters of the Pacific bound rivers. The aboriginal fishermen developed many techniques to trap the tasty salmon! Weirs or nets were constructed in shallow water to block the path of the fish. Screened nets were strategically placed at the top of waterfalls, so salmon jumping over the waterfall were caught as they fell back. Dip nets would allow the fisherman to stand on a ledge above the stream and scoop the fish out of the swiftly flowing waters. Spears with two prongs were also used to stab fish as they swam upstream.

Most of the salmon caught was smoked over a slow open fire, and stored in underground pits lined with birch bark, for winter provisions. Some of the salmon was boiled in watertight baskets made of split spruce and cedar roots. After cooling, the oil from the fish was skimmed off the top and kept to make fish pemmican, a combination of powdered dried fish, and Saskatoon berries.

The First Nations of the Plateau

The First Nations of the Plateau used bow and arrows and spears and knives as weapons for hunting. They also used nets to trap waterfowl. A net stretched above duck feeding grounds would trap the birds as they took flight. Deadfall traps were also a method used to capture larger game. Deep pits would be dug in a deer run and hidden with a blanket of twigs and leaves. A deer running along the path would fall into the pit and be unable to free itself.

Along with game, wild vegetables were an important part of the members of the First Nations of the Plateau's diet. Camas, a wild lily bulb was an important but dangerous root. The blue flowered Camas was edible but the white flowered Camas was poisonous! To protect themselves, the natives harvested these bulbs only when the lily was in bloom. Digging tools were made of deer antlers or mountain sheep horns, and made harvesting wild onions, skunk cabbage and water parsnip roots less difficult.

Cooking these roots was left to the older females of the tribe, as it needed know-how. A shallow pit was dug, and filled with hot stones. Once the ground around the stones was heated, the stones were removed and a layer of bulbs and leaves were placed in the hole. Finally, earth and skins were laid on top and the bulbs were left to cook overnight. Camas bulbs prepared in this way could last for months after cooling and drying.

Berry cakes were made from Saskatoon berries, salmon berries, raspberries and blueberries, all gathered from surrounding areas. The berries were dried on racks covered with cedar and leaves. What tasty treats for the cold winter!

The bark of the evergreen and poplar trees was gathered in the spring as the sap rose in the trees. It was scraped off in long slivers and dried. This sweet orange tasting bark was like candy!

Travel by the First Nations of the Plateau was usually done on foot. The Fraser River and the Thompson River, the main waterways in the area, were swift with many rapids and waterfalls, so they were hard to navigate. The Thompson First Nations did however create three types of canoes. The birch bark canoe, the cedar dugout, and skin covered with wooden frames.

Travel was not necessary if food was not an issue. The Carrier tribe lived on the salmon stored from their fishing expeditions, and therefore did not need to hunt during the winter. The tribe that did not have the luxury of stored food and had to hunt in winter used toboggans, some made from the leg skins of the moose. Dogs were used to pack heavy loads.

The First Nations of the Plateau

Winter houses of the Interior Salish were very different from the buffalo hide teepees made by the other First Nations groups. The Salish dug holes in the gravel close to riverbeds. These pits were lined with spruce boughs and a teepee like cone was built over the pit. The cone was covered with more boughs and the earth that had been excavated from the pit. A log was then fashioned into steps, and placed in the opening. The structure was 5-15 metres wide and 2-3 metres deep. Many families lived in the dwelling, and met around a central fire to cook and chat. Dried food was stored outside the pit in boxes on poles or in bark-lined holes. In summer the Salish lived in lodges covered with mats made from rushes.

Other tribes of the First Nations of the Plateau built homes of cedar slab, or lean-tos made from spruce bark. The cedar slab homes had roofs that slanted straight down to the ground, giving them an identifiable shape. The double lean-tos looked like two tents facing each other.

The clothing of the First Nations of the Plateau consisted of buckskin shirts, breechcloths, leggings and moccasins for the men, while the women wore a longer shirt. Robes of rabbit or groundhog fur woven together made warm winter wear. Sometimes the garments were decorated with red clay along the seam lines, or ornamental fringes.

The First Nations of the Plateau had shamans who were believed to control the weather, and heal the sick. Some tribes looked to the supernatural for guidance, and underwent fasting and seclusion in search of spiritual visions. The tribes held festivals during the winter, where storytelling and dancing was an important part of the celebrations.

The Lillooet and the Shuswap danced with masks to tell the vision quest that one of their youth had been on. The dance told of the guardian spirit that possessed the young man or woman.

The First Nations of the Plateau

Fill in the chart below:

Principal Tribes:	
Transportation:	
Housing:	
Uses of Bark:	
Hunting:	
Clothing:	
Ceremonies and Beliefs:	

The First Nations of the Plateau

Use the word box to find the missing word in the paragraph.

The Plains First Nations lived in a _____

and sometimes _____ environment. The

valley between the Rocky Mountains and the

_____ ranges had many different regions.

The south end of the area was a, _____

with sagebrush, _____ and cactus, while

the north end was _____ and abundant

with _____ such as moose and deer.

Between these two _____ was an area of

rushing rivers and waterfalls. _____ ran

_____ in the spring in these waters.

Word Box

diverse	semi-desert
coastal	wildlife
forested	difficult
expanses	plentiful
rattlesnakes	salmon

The First Nations of the Plateau

B	U	C	K	S	K	I	N	X	C	M	O	O	S	E
F	D	A	F	G	H	F	J	R	L	T	Y	I	U	C
E	C	N	K	O	P	I	Q	A	U	B	S	J	B	A
S	N	O	W	T	Y	S	U	T	C	A	C	U	T	M
T	D	E	E	R	J	H	S	T	G	H	A	K	E	A
I	B	M	K	L	N	O	M	L	A	S	R	J	R	S
V	T	R	A	D	E	P	Q	E	W	A	I	H	R	N
A	G	H	L	O	D	G	E	S	D	L	B	S	A	A
L	N	F	M	C	P	B	F	N	M	I	O	I	N	G
S	A	N	S	A	A	N	V	A	U	S	U	G	E	A
H	T	A	R	R	W	M	H	K	V	H	F	A	A	N
I	L	M	E	R	S	Y	D	E	S	E	R	T	N	A
R	H	A	V	I	U	L	I	L	L	O	O	E	T	K
T	A	H	I	E	H	Y	A	N	E	T	O	O	K	O
S	T	S	R	R	S	E	L	B	A	T	E	G	E	V

BUCKSKIN	CACTUS	CAMAS
CANOE	CARIBOU	CARRIER
DEER	DESERT	KOOTENAY
LAKE	LILLOOET	FISH
LODGES	MOOSE	OKANAGAN
RATTLESNAKE	RIVERS	SALISH
SALMON	SHAMAN	SHIRTS
SHUSWAP	SUBTERRANEAN	TAGISH
TAHLTAN	TRADE	VEGETABLES
FESTIVALS		

The First Nations of the Plateau

Using information from the story and your own ideas tell how the First Nations of the Plains and the First Nations of the Plateau were the same and how were they different. Give examples.

_____

_____

_____

_____

_____

_____

_____

_____

_____

_____

_____

_____

_____

_____

_____

_____

_____

The Pacific Coast First Nations

Did you know the tribes of the Pacific Coast First nations were different from the other tribes in Canada because they had a very organized social structure? There were nobles, commoners and slaves in the tribes. The upper class was special just because they were born into a specific family.

There were six principal tribes of the Pacific Coast First Nations. The Haida were the only members that spoke the Haida language and lived in the Queen Charlotte Islands. Across from the Queen Charlotte Islands on the mainland lived the Tsimshian. They were separated into three groups who all spoke the Tsimshian language. The Salishan language family lived along the east coast of Vancouver Island and on the mainland at the mouth of the Columbia River. Between these northern and southern tribes lived the Kwakiutl and the Bella Coola, who also belonged to the Salishan language family.

Some of these tribes traced their line of decent or their family tree through the mother, while others traced their lineage through the father. In any case these family trees were important, because they determined who got the best sites for fishing, hunting, wood and bark collecting and shellfish gathering. It also determined the right to wear specific ceremonial masks, and dance certain dances.

Each group had its own crest, usually of an animal or spiritual being thought to be their originator. These crests were sometimes called totems and were used everywhere possible! They were painted on homes, clothing, and beds, tattooed on bodies, painted on faces and woven into formal clothing. They were carved into plates, spoons, masks and storage containers.

This art form has made the Pacific Coast First Nations well recognized. One of the most recognized art forms around the world is the totem pole. The totem pole is a depiction of the symbols belonging to the ancestry of the tribe. It is carved on huge red cedar poles and shows forms of humans and animals sitting atop of each other, reaching into the sky.

There were many kinds of totem poles. The memorial poles were built when a chief died and his replacement carved the totem pole to commemorate him. The house portal pole was erected at the door of the home, telling all those who entered the inhabitant's lineage. These poles had large holes at their base that acted like a doorway.

The social structure of the Pacific Coast First Nations determined things like who would be chief of the village and who would earn very little in the tribe. The lowest person in the tribe was the most distant relation to the chief, but he could lift his status if he became particularly good at a skill such as mask carving or canoe making. Slaves were used to perform tasks such as gathering wood or digging for clams.

Fishing was the main form of food gathering of the Pacific Coast First Nations. Dip nets made from nettle fibres were attached to wooden frames. These nets were used to catch salmon, herring and smelt. Gill nets were also used. Gill nets catch a fish when it tries to swim though the holes. The fish gets caught by the gills as it tries to pull its head out. Harpooning, trapping and baited hooks were also techniques used to catch fish.

The Pacific Coast First Nations

The women of the tribes were responsible for catching shellfish, such as clams, periwinkles, abalone, mussels and oysters. They used a hardwood stick to pry the shells open and prepare the shellfish. Fish was the staple food for the Pacific Coast First Nations. The fish was dried or smoked and stored for later meals. In season, they would also gather berries, sometimes preserving them in oil for the coming winter.

Oil was an important part of the Pacific Coast First Nation's diet. It made the dried fish easier to eat, kept the berries preserved and helped make up for the lack of starch in the native diet. One of the best sources of oil was the eulachon, a fish about 15 centimetres long and packed with oil. Its nickname was the candle fish, because if lit, it burned end to end like a candle!

Collecting the oil was an interesting chore! Women would place the fish in large barrels and add hot stones to quicken the process of rotting. When the fish were rotten enough, they squeezed the rotting fish against their chests to allow the oil to run into bags made from sea mammal's intestines! The Tsimshian and Nisga tribes controlled the oil production and traded it to other tribes. The routes they took into the interior of British Columbia are still known today as the grease trails!

 The Pacific Coast First Nations traveled by water in canoes made of red cedar. This wood was abundant on the west coast, and the aboriginal people of this area used it for many items. Cedar is a soft beautiful wood with a lovely smell. Aboriginal west coast tribes used it to make masks, totem poles, containers, houses and canoes. The soft inner bark was used to make clothing, baskets, napkins and tablecloths! But it was canoe-making that was thought to be a sacred skill.

The canoes they built were called "dugouts". The Haida made canoes that were high in the front and back. These canoes could glide over the ocean waters without being swamped by waves. The Haida expertise in building these beautiful canoes made them admired by all west coast nations. Sometimes carved figures were secured to the front of the boats. The Haida would use their canoes to trade with other tribes.

It was important that the canoes be seaworthy because the hunters went to sea to catch whales. The harpooner sat behind the raised bow with a huge harpoon made of yew wood. It had a spear head made from shell that had been sharpened into a point, and attached with spruce gum, between two barb-like elk antlers. When the harpoon was thrust into the whale, the spearhead would detach from the wooden pole and a twisted rope of spruce root would uncoil. Tied along the rope were inflated sealskins. These sealskins acted like balloons and made it difficult for the whale to dive into the depths of the sea, pulling the boat with it.

Once a whale was sited in the ocean, the canoe of hunters would carefully glide up along side the whale, and the standing harpooner would sink the harpoon as deep as he could into the whale. If the whale swam into the ocean during this wild ride, it could take days to tow it back into the shore. Returning hunt parties were met with great enthusiasm. A festival called all the chiefs of the tribes to the beach. The whale blubber was divided among the visitors in order of their rank.

The Pacific Coast First Nations

The Pacific Coast First Nations built village sites that lasted for many years. In fact, some sites have been around for 4,000 years! The villages were usually built on the shores of bays and inlets, away from the ocean. Thirty lodges in the village could support about 700 people.

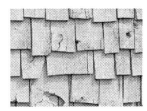 Just as cedar was used for canoes, totem poles and other utensils, it was also used for building homes. The Haida, Tsimshian, and Kwakiutl built large houses held up by large carved and decorated poles at the front and back. The roof was built of cedar planks that overlapped. The walls were planks of cedar fitted into sills. The large rectangular house had an oval doorway in the side that faced the beach.

The Nootka, Bella Coola and Salish built their homes slightly differently because they were more mobile, moving from fishing site to fishing site. The houses had outer walls that were easily disconnected and re-built by attaching to new wooden frames.

The insides of these houses were large with places for many families. Most sleeping accommodations were platforms along the walls. Each family was able to have its own hearth for cooking. Around the hearth the members of the families sat on mats woven from cedar bark. Wooden chests were common and were used for storing possessions such as oil, ceremonial masks, clothing, and whale blubber. Often the clan crests were carved into the tops and sides, making them true works of art.

While cedar was a common wood for carving, it did not make good food containers. The fragrant oils in the wood transferred to the food. Most food containers were simple troughs, dug out of alder.

Because of the temperate west coast climate, the First Nations of the Pacific Coast did not often wear clothing. In the rainy season, tribes wore variations of a cape. Theses capes were woven from bark or roots striped to produce a soft fibre.

All Pacific Coast Peoples believed in the "salmon people". Salmon was so important in their lives that they believed salmon were really supernatural people who lived in the waters. When the salmon runs began these people would transform themselves into fish and return each year to feed human beings.

Haida Pacific Coast shamans wore their hair long and used bone tubes to take away illnesses. Other tribes made up dramas, dances and mimes to capture lost souls.

Winter was a favourite time for ceremonies. Secret societies performed the ritual dramas and dances. Carved masks played an important role in the festivals, as did puppets and fire. The potlatch was a ceremony shared by all the Pacific Coast First Nations. The feast was one of dancing and presents were given to invited guests. The chief who held the potlatch was considered high in social status, and the more material things he distributed, the wealthier he was believed to be!

The Pacific Coast First Nations

Fill in the chart below:

Principal Tribes:	
Transportation:	
Housing:	
Uses of salmon:	
Significance of the totem pole:	
Clothing:	
Ceremonies and Beliefs:	

The Pacific Coast First Nations

E	L	D	N	A	C	V	B	N	A	G	S	C	W	T
H	A	I	D	A	T	H	D	Y	B	N	E	O	H	U
C	O	M	M	O	N	E	R	S	W	I	V	O	A	O
S	P	N	T	L	S	F	K	A	A	V	A	L	L	G
B	H	E	A	T	I	W	F	N	K	R	L	A	E	U
S	M	E	S	K	A	O	A	C	A	A	S	K	S	D
A	K	E	L	K	S	I	K	G	S	C	V	I	U	H
B	R	E	I	L	H	T	N	O	H	C	A	L	U	E
C	E	U	E	S	F	D	I	N	A	M	J	W	X	N
S	T	L	M	N	E	I	O	G	N	F	L	B	F	I
L	L	I	L	L	A	O	S	S	P	I	R	I	T	S
B	S	E	L	A	T	H	Y	H	S	E	L	O	P	G
T	T	I	B	K	H	S	I	L	A	S	C	I	Q	A
N	K	O	A	O	Q	S	A	L	M	O	N	N	Q	A
S	G	W	C	A	N	O	E	F	M	R	A	D	E	C

BELLA

CARVING

COOLA

EULACHON

KWAKIUTL

NOOTKA

SALISH

SKEENA

SPIRITS

WAKASHAN

CANDLE

CEDAR

CRESTS

GITSKAN

NISGA

OIL

SALMON

SKILLED

TOTEM

WHALES

CANOE

COMMONERS

DUGOUT

HAIDA

NOBELS

POLES

SHELLFISH

SLAVES

TSIMSHIAN

The Pacific Coast First Nations

Using information from the story, and your own ideas, explain the social structure of the Pacific Coast First Nations. Do you think this was a good system? Why or why not.

_____

_____

_____

_____

_____

_____

_____

_____

_____

_____

_____

_____

_____

_____

_____

_____

_____

Art Project: Create your own crest using an animal or spiritual being that the Pacific Coast Nations might have thought to be their originator.

The First Nations of
the Mackenzie and Yukon River Basin

Did you know the twelve tribes of the Mackenzie and Yukon River basins spoke the Athapaskan language? The Chipewyan controlled the biggest territory. This territory ranged from the Churchill River to the Great Slave Lake. South of this area were the Beaver who lived in the Peace River basin. The Slave controlled the area west of Great Slave Lake to the Mackenzie River. The Yellowknife occupied east of Great Slave Lake to Great Bear Lake, and the Dogrib controlled the land southwest of this region between the two lakes.

The Hare lived to the west of the Great Bear Lake and the Kutchin occupied the basins of the Pelly and Porcupine rivers. What we know today as the southern Yukon was the home of the Han and Tutchone. South of them were the Kaska and the Mountain. Today's northern Alberta was the territory of the Sekani.

The region covered by the First Nations of the Mackenzie and Yukon River basins was huge, but the game was scarce. This influenced their way of life considerably. They wandered the region following the migration of the animals they hunted. This way of life is called **semi-nomadic**.

In the northern regions much of the land remains frozen all year round. This is called **permafrost** and only the very top or surface of the land thaws. A great deal of the region is covered in tundra. Tundra is the layer of permafrost out of which the vegetation grows. It is above the treeline, making fuel and protection hard to find.

The people were busy trying to survive this **harsh** climate, so therefore social groups were simple. Each tribe was divided into a few family groups who hunted and worked together. A leader was chosen as the need arose. A good caribou hunter would lead the tribe during the caribou hunt, while the best warrior would lead the tribe during a raid.

Moose were the main source of **game** in the region. Calling the moose using a bark horn, or rubbing an antler against a tree, **threatened** the male moose's territory, causing it to challenge this threat. When the moose appeared, the hunter would use a bow and arrow to kill it.

The best time for moose hunting was when the snow was deep and crusty. The moose would fall through the crusted snow and tire quickly. The hunter on snowshoes was no match and the moose was easily hunted down.

The Chipewyan and the Yellowknife followed large herds of caribou. When the caribou approached the rivers or waterways, they chased the animals into the water. Hunters in canoes would spear the animals in the water. They would also **corral** the animals in fenced areas where they could be easily speared or shot with bows and arrows. The Kutchin built corrals on the permafrost, a difficult and time consuming task. They took care of their fences and would will them to their children.

The First Nations of
the Mackenzie and Yukon River Basin

In winter meat **preservation** was not a problem, but **scavenger** animals were! Most storage was in a high tree whenever possible. The tree bark would be stripped away, causing a slippery trunk that animals could not scale. In the summer meat was dried in the sun and pounded into powder to be used to make pemmican.

Fishing was important to the First Nations of the Mackenzie and Yukon River basins. The Hare did not fish as much as the other tribes. In winter in the northern regions, holes were cut into the ice and fish were speared. Tribes who lived along the river edges fished using nets and lines made from willow bark strips. Fishhooks were made from bones, wood, antlers or claws.

Moose and caribou hide was most often used for clothing. The women prepared the hide using different techniques for **tanning** the summer clothing and winter clothing. For winter the fur was left on the skins, for extra warmth. Caribou fur is shaped like a straw, and the heat would be captured in its hollow core. Summer clothing was scraped until all the fur was removed and treated with animal brains, making the skins soft and workable. Caribou and moose sinew made strong thread.

Homes were designed to be easy to put up and take down, because of the semi-nomadic lifestyle of the tribes. Lodges were often **pitched** beside another family in order to share a common fire. Coverings were usually hide, spruce boughs, moss, or snow for **insulation**.

Birch bark canoes were built in the northern areas, when the sap rose in the trees in the spring. The birch trees were not as big as the ones in the east, so many seams had to be sealed with spruce gum in order to make the canoe waterproof. In the south, huge spruce trees were striped of their bark in one piece, making canoes. The ends were sewn together with spruce root and made waterproof with spruce gum. Ribs of wood strips shaped to take the form of the canoe were placed on the bottoms of the canoes to give them strength.

Toboggans were the main method of transportation for the First Nations of the Mackenzie and Yukon River basin. They built their sleds from green wood that was steamed and shaped with a curl in the front to prevent the toboggan from digging into the snow. Families carried their possessions **lashed** to toboggans across the snow-covered lands.

This region was covered in snow from September to May, so snowshoes were an important means of transportation. These snowshoes were different from other tribes across Canada, because they were longer and the tips were bent up to prevent the snowshoe from becoming caught on twigs under the snow.

The First Nations of
the Mackenzie and Yukon River Basin

Guardian spirits were a common belief. These spirits were sent to protect the people in hard times and were often **obtained** during vision quests. Shamans were highly revered and had great powers. It was believed they could predict the weather and tell where the game could be found.

In the Kutchin the shaman was often an elderly woman. She would burn an arrow on a moose shoulder blade, and the ashes would tell the way to the animal hunt. A blanket would be thrown over the old lady and the burning arrow. If she smelled meat burning, the hunt would be successful!

Hunters treated their kill with respect, believing that the animal possessed a soul. **Rituals** were followed when disposing of the bones and unused parts. Some animals were considered special ceremonial animals. The lynx, wolverine, and wolf were among those.

Festivals were times when dancing, singing, drumming and races showed-off strength, and feasting! A special festival took place at the winter solstice and the new moon.
Special memorial feasts for the dead were held on the first anniversary of the death of the person.

The Slave and the Chipewayan believed the soul took a special journey after death. The soul crossed a lake in a stone canoe. If the dead person had a good life, the canoe went to a land rich in game and firewood! If he had lived a wicked life, his stone canoe would sink and he would be forced to live in the depths of the icy water forever.

Brainwork:

- Create a silent ritual to reenact the way hunters might have disposed bones and unused parts of animals. Introduce the ritual by explaining its importance.

- The Slave and the Chipewayan believed the soul took a special journey after death. Write a story about a soul's journey while crossing the lake.

The First Nations of
the Mackenzie and Yukon River Basin

Fill in the chart below:

Principal Tribes:	
Transportation:	
Housing:	
Hunting:	
Clothing:	
Ceremonies and Beliefs:	

The First Nations of
the Mackenzie and Yukon River Basin

Find the definitions of the bolded words in the story.

semi-nomadic	animals that are hunted
permafrost	to pen or capture animals
harsh	wandering around in search of food as the seasons changed
game	the frozen ground under the tundra
threatened	severe and difficult
corral	keeping it from rotting
preservation	tied to
scavenger	to place something at risk
tanning	hunting
pitched	helps to keep the cold or heat out
insulation	curing hide to make it wearable
lashed	to build a tent
obtained	a ceremony or custom
rituals	to acquire something

The First Nations of
the Mackenzie and Yukon River Basin

Using information from the story, answer the following questions.

1. Why was game scarce in this region?

_____

_____

_____

2. How did this scarcity of game influence the life-style of the First Nations of the Mackenzie and Yukon River basins?

_____

_____

_____

3. How was a leader of the tribe chosen?

_____

_____

_____

4. Explain how meat was preserved.

_____

_____

_____

5. How did the First Nations of the Mackenzie and Yukon River basins fish?

_____

_____

_____

The First Nations of
the Mackenzie and Yukon River Basin

6. Describe the methods of transportation used by the First Nations of the Mackenzie and Yukon River basins.

_____

_____

_____

7. Using information from the story and your own ideas tell how permafrost effected the First Nations of the Mackenzie and Yukon River basins.

_____

_____

_____

_____

_____

_____

_____

_____

_____

_____

_____

_____

The Nations of the Mackenzie and Yukon River Basin

E	O	N	A	C	S	N	N	F	S	T	S	B	O	W
R	F	J	I	E	A	I	Z	E	H	S	O	I	N	G
A	G	I	K	H	A	A	I	A	E	O	L	X	X	P
H	S	A	N	T	C	N	D	E	E	R	S	K	I	N
B	N	E	N	K	O	T	R	C	P	F	T	U	S	D
I	E	U	O	M	W	A	U	U	S	A	I	O	E	O
F	O	A	E	H	I	O	U	K	K	M	C	B	E	G
M	U	R	V	D	S	G	L	Q	I	R	E	I	N	R
C	E	R	S	E	D	W	R	L	N	E	S	R	O	I
C	T	U	N	D	R	A	O	A	E	P	O	A	H	B
C	H	I	P	E	W	Y	A	N	T	Y	O	C	C	S
S	N	A	G	G	O	B	O	T	S	O	M	N	T	L
L	A	V	I	T	S	E	F	W	O	R	R	A	U	A
R	E	T	N	I	W	S	P	E	A	R	S	Y	T	V
X	F	I	S	H	I	N	G	N	A	M	A	H	S	E

ARROW   BEAVER   BOW
CANOE   CARIBOU   CEREMONIES
CHIPEWYAN   DEERSKIN   DOGRIB
FESTIVAL   FISHING   FUR
HAN   HARE   KUTCHIN
MIGRATORY   MOOSE   MOUNTAIN
PERMAFROST   RAIDS   YELLOWKNIFE
SHAMAN   SHEEPSKIN   SLAVE
SNOWSHOES   SOLSTICE   SPEARS
TOBOGGANS   TUNDRA   TUTCHONE
WINTER

The Europeans

Did you know the arrival of the European settlers in Canada changed the people of the First Nations forever? Before the discovery of the "new world" the aboriginal way of life was based on the gathering of belongings and the right to perform rituals, songs and dances. The chief was responsible for the well being of his tribe. Trading with other villages was a way of showing the wealth of the village. The First Nations People used the natural resources in their area. They made extra goods from the things available in their region in order to trade with other groups. Traders would be sent out to barter for goods not found in their area. The goods received were for the whole group, and individual wealth was not even thought of. Partnerships between groups were sealed with the giving and receiving of gifts.

All this changed with the arrival of the Europeans. They thought only of individual needs, instead of doing things that were in the best interest of the whole group! Furs were traded for goods. The French traded things like mirrors or ironworks. These items were thought to be treasures by aboriginal groups. This caused fighting between those who were not trading with the French. Soon aboriginal groups had left their traditional ways of life to concentrate on fur trapping in order to gain European supplies. This caused a dependency on the European fur companies.

Aboriginal laws were rooted in ideas of healing and treatment. The community was important and laws were meant to protect the group. Shamans were an important part of the healing process, and when someone broke the laws of the tribe, it was believed that they needed healing. These healers were in charge of spirit, body and mind, and encouraged lawbreakers to change their ways.

The shamans and elders advised the lawbreakers. These meetings were known as Justice Circles. Basic consequences were given for the unacceptable behaviour. If the crime was serious enough to affect the whole village, whippings or banishment could be decided upon.

European laws were based upon repayment and punishment. The First Nations People were made to follow European laws. This was an attempt to destroy a way of life that the Europeans saw as savage and undeveloped.

The shaman healers learned that herbs and plants had certain effects on the human body. They taught many of the first explorers cures using plant and herbs. Spruce bud tea helped the early settlers get rid of scurvy. Sweetgrass was an important herb in the native traditions. Burned, it would bring health and balance to the patient. The shaman treated toothaches, broken bones and coughs successfully. Over 500 drugs used by aboriginal people are part of our modern drugs today!

The Europeans

Europeans were ignorant to the healing values of these herbs. They made the aboriginal people reject the shaman's ways. The Europeans brought with them diseases the native people had never been exposed to before. Smallpox, measles, and tuberculosis were previously unheard of, and epidemics of these diseases devastated entire villages.

There were many common beliefs in the religions of the First Nations in Canada. There was an understanding that all things, living or not, had a spirit. Ceremonies and rituals were devoted to these spirits. The spirits needed to be made happy in order to maintain harmony within the tribe. The sun and the sky were important elements in their beliefs.

Vision quests were a part of growing up for young boys. Fasting and prayer would encourage an animals guide to appear to the youngster. The animal guide explained his future to the boy, and often became his guide for life.

The shaman was the man or woman who was the religious leader. Shaman interpreted dreams, communicated with the spirits and kept the tribe healthy. Often they were the most powerful members of the tribe.

The French explorers came to Canada with Catholic missionaries. The missionaries believed the Aboriginal People needed to be converted to Christianity, so they gave special trading privileges to those who converted to Christianity. As trade became a more important part within the tribes, traditional ceremonies began to be abandoned for Christian celebrations. The shaman's power was replaced by Catholic beliefs and the belief in the natural world was almost lost.

Aboriginal children were taught the ways of their tribes. They learned the oral traditions, history, life skills and spiritual beliefs of their ancestors. Boys were taught skills such as fishing, wood crafting or tool making. Girls were trained in the construction of homes, preservation and preparation of food and clothing. Some children were trained to be shaman.

Some tribes believed it would be to their benefit to have their children educated in the ways of the Europeans. They thought this would give them a trading advantage. They sent their children to the missionary schools, believing the children could remain part of their native culture.

The missionaries had different opinions. They established residential schools. The government and the missionaries thought the children should break-off their ties with their tribes. The aboriginal children were forbidden to speak their native language. They were made to eat unfamiliar food, wear unfamiliar clothing and live indoors, after  having lived their lives outdoors! After many years in residential schools, they did not fit into their aboriginal group anymore. They did not fit into the European groups because of their ethnic background. Everyone rejected them.

In 1996 the Royal Commission on Aboriginal Peoples said the government and churches should apologize to the children they took away from their families. The government gave $350,000,000.00 to start the Aboriginal Healing Foundation to help the people who suffered as children. Today, there are First Nations schools that educate Aboriginal children in the ways of their ancestors.

The Europeans

Using information from the story, answer the following questions.

1. Explain how the arrival of the Europeans in Canada changed Aboriginal life.

_____

_____

_____

2. How were Aboriginal laws and European laws different?

_____

_____

_____

3. What was a justice circle?

_____

_____

_____

4. How did the shaman healers help European settlers?

_____

_____

_____

5. How did the religious beliefs of the Aboriginal people and the Europeans differ?

_____

_____

_____

6. What happened to children who went to the residential schools?

_____

_____

_____

The Europeans

7. What has the Canadian government done to say they are sorry for the treatment of Aboriginal children?

_____

_____

_____

8. Using information from the story and your own ideas, explain why the Europeans thought it was a good idea to change the way of life of the Aboriginal people of Canada.

_____

_____

_____

_____

_____

_____

_____

_____

_____

_____

_____

9. Do you think the Europeans had the right to try to change the way of life of the Aboriginal people of Canada? Explain your thinking.

_____

_____

_____

_____

_____

A Few Famous People of the First Nations

CHIEF DAN GEORGE - ACTOR

Chief Dan George was born in 1899 in British Columbia. He was a member of the Salish Band of Burrard Inlet. His Salish name was Geswanouth Slahoot. He worked as a longshoreman and a logger until he was 60 years old. He was Chief of the Tsleil-Waututh Band from 1951 to 1963.

He began acting on stage and in Canadian television in 1959. His Hollywood film career began as the role of an Aboriginal who adopts a character played by Dustin Hoffman in the movie Little Big Man. In 1970, he received an Academy Award nomination for this role and a New York Film Critics Award for Best Actor. He also worked with Clint Eastwood in the 1976 movie The Outlaw Josey Wales. Dan George spent much of his life trying to improve non-Aboriginal people's understanding of Aboriginal people. Dan George died in 1981.

GRAHAM GREENE - ACTOR

Graham Green won an Academy Award nomination for his role in *Dance's With Wolves*, Kevin Costner's film. He has performed on stage, television and in film. He is famous for his role as Mr. Crabby tree in the *Adventures of Dudley Dragon*, as well as appearances on *North of 60, Murder She Wrote, The Great Detective, Thunderheart, Die Hard 3* and *Northern Exposure,* to name only a few. In 1997, Graham Greene received a National Aboriginal Achievement Award for his work as an actor.

MARY TWO-AXE EARLEY -ACTIVIST

Mary Two-Axe Earley was a Mohawk woman from the Kahnawake reserve near Montreal. Her parents taught her about the traditional equality between Mohawk men and women. For more than 27 years, Mary Two-Axe Earley fought to have the government change a part of the Indian Act that was unfair to Aboriginal women. The Indian Act stated that if an Aboriginal woman married a non-aboriginal man she lost her status as an Aboriginal. The Indian Act was changed in 1985 by a law called Bill C-31. Now Aboriginal women who lost their rights by marrying non-Aboriginal men regained their rights.

Mary Two-Axe Earley was given the Persons Award for helping women in Canada, the Governor General's Award, the Order of Quebec and an honorary Doctor of Law degree from York University. In 1996, Two-AxeEarley was recognized with a National Aboriginal Achievement Award.

BRIAN TROTTIER - HOCKEY

Brian Trottier is an Aboriginal who at the age of 17 played his first professional game and later won the NHL's "Rookie Of The Year" award! He also won the Hart Trophy (Most Valuable Player) and in 1980 the Conn Smythe Trophy (Most Valuable Player in the Stanley Cup Playoffs). He was born in Val Marie, Saskatchewan, to a Cree/Chippewa father. He and his team, the New York Islanders, won the Stanley Cup four years in a row, beginning in 1980. He has been inducted into the Hockey Hall of Fame, and received a National Aboriginal Achievement Award, for hockey.

🍁 Faye Heavyshields

Time Frame: 30 minutes

Faye Heavyshields is a contemporary First Nations artist. She was born on the Stand Off Reserve in southern Alberta, and graduated from the Alberta College of Art in 1985. She produced a famous sculpture of six pairs of golden high heel shoes arranged in a circle. You can see a photograph of this sculpture at www.mcmichael.com

MOTIVATION:
In this activity, students will collect common articles and change them into a modern day contemporary sculpture.

MATERIALS:
- Collection of common articles (buttons, clothes pegs, crayons, etc.)
- White glue
- Newsprint (or paper toweling, or toilet paper)
- Water
- Spray paint or acrylic paint
- Paintbrushes
- Masking tape

WHAT TO DO:
1. Demonstrate for the students how to use the masking tape to join the common articles together to form a sculpture;
2. Explain how to mix equal parts white glue and water;
3. Add shredded newsprint (or other suggestions) to the water and glue to form a modeling compound;
4. Demonstrate how to apply modeling compound over the sculpture, covering the masking tape and shaping the sculpture, until satisfied with the creation;
5. Let the sculpture dry completely before applying paint.

Alex Janvier

The First Nations People of Canada have been creating art for many, many years. When non-native people came to North America, they collected and traded tools made by native people. The non-native people did not always understand the beauty of the Native Art, but artists like Alex Janvier helped to make Native Art an important part of Canada.

Alex Janvier was born in 1935. He was raised on the Le Goffe Reserve in Cold Lake Alberta. He studied at the Alberta College of Art and graduated in 1960. Alex Janvier paints pictures that seem to flow across the canvas. He likes to draw about the traditional native beadwork designs and many of the things that have happened to the First Nations people in Canada when he paints. You can see examples of his art at www.mcmichael.com

Many beautiful designs are found in Native beadwork. Porcupine quills were dyed and sewn to leather bands or birch bark. Use the following activity to create designs that emulate this beadwork.

Beadwork Designs

MATERIALS:
- Flat toothpicks
- Food colouring or jelly powder crystals (added to small quantities of water to create a dye bath for the toothpicks).
- Glue
- Strips of brown construction paper (bracelets)

WHAT TO DO:
1. Before beginning the activity, soak the toothpicks in food colouring or diluted jelly powder bath;
2. Allow toothpicks to dry;
3. After viewing examples of native beadwork, distribute strips of brown construction paper to be used as bracelets;
4. Model for the children how to create a design on their construction paper, like a bird, tree or any traditional native picture by breaking the toothpicks to fit the design;
5. Next have children glue toothpick pieces making the design using colours of their choice;
6. The teacher may wish to read with the class several native stories and legends to act as inspiration for the children.

Teacher Tip: Lay toothpicks across the construction paper bracelets so when bent around the wrist, the toothpicks will not break.

Find legends at: http://www.ainc-inac.gc.ca/ks/english/index_e.html

Bob Boyer

Bob Boyer is a Metis artist born near Prince Albert, Saskatchewan. He graduated from the University of Regina in 1971. While Bob Boyer has worked in a variety of media, he is best known for his "Blanket Statements". He uses blankets as a surface on which to create traditional designs of the Plains Cree people. See examples of Bob Boyer's work at: www.mcmichael.com

Painting on Fabric

Time Frame: 40 minutes

MOTIVATION:

After examining Boyer's art, have the children create their own "Blanket Statement". If fabric is not readily available, brown lunch bags may be substituted.

MATERIALS:
- Scrap fabric
- Paint
- Geometric templates (these may be made from cardboard)
- Brushes
- Water
- Masking tape
- Permanent markers

WHAT TO DO:
1. Demonstrate for the children how to trace geometric designs on a scrap on fabric using the permanent markers;
2. Using the masking tape, secure the fabric on all sides to a hard surface such as a table or easel; (if using a table, a pad of newspaper slightly smaller than the fabric should be secured to the table to absorb paint bleeding through)
3. Carefully paint in the geometric designs and allow to dry.

Norval Morrisseau

Copper Thunderbird or Norval Morrisseau, was born March 14, 1932 near Thunderbay Ontario. Morrisseau has the distinction of being the only Canadian artist to be asked to exhibit his work in the Paris French Revolution bicentennial in 1989. He has received the order of Canada, and was elected to the Royal Canadian Academy of Arts. He is the founder of the Canadian originated Woodland School. The Woodland School focuses on the spiritual images, or "x-rays" of the subject's feelings or insides. See an example of Morrisseau's art at: www.kinderart.com/multic/norval.shtml

Native Woodland Paintings

Time Frame: 40 minutes

MOTIVATION:

This activity is a wonderful follow-up to a discussion on feelings, and expressions. Morrisseau contended that his paintings showed not only the outside, but the energy inside his subjects as well.

MATERIALS:

- Enlarged tracer
- Markers
- Drawing paper

WHAT TO DO:

1. Demonstrate for the children how to trace the animal of their choice on the drawing paper;
2. Ask the children how the animal might feel, and what symbols would represent their energy;
3. Draw their suggestion inside the animal;
4. Have children experiment with representational drawings of the feelings of their animal.

Tracers

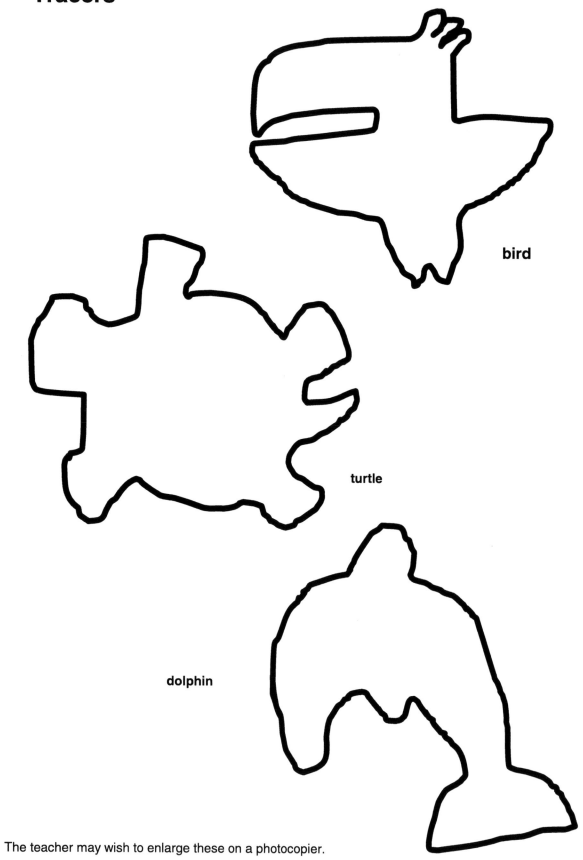

bird

turtle

dolphin

The teacher may wish to enlarge these on a photocopier.

Artists of the First Nations

You may wish to see some of the art that inspired the ideas in the art section of this unit. Check them out at:

http://www.ainc-inac.gc.ca/ks/english/index_e.html

www.mcmichael.com

www.kinderart.com/multic/norval.shtml

Other interesting websites about First Nations:

http://collections.ic.gc.ca/heirloom_series/volume2/volume2.htm

http://www.rom.on.ca/digs/longhouse/index.html

http://xist.com/ROM-MCQ/E/index.htm

http://www.pma.edmonton.ab.ca/gallery/peoples/galtour.htm

http://www.civilization.ca/aborig/aborige.asp

http://www.carnegiemuseums.org/cmnh/exhibits/north-south-east-west/index.html

http://www.civilisations.ca/vmnf/premieres_nations/en/index.html

Canada's First Nations: Unit Test

Name _____

1. The Woodland tribes had their own territory for:

☐ paddling their canoes.

☐ hunting and fishing.

☐ building residences.

☐ making long houses.

2. The Woodland First Nations had a great respect for the animals they hunted,

☐ and many of their ceremonies and beliefs were connected to this respect.

☐ and they did not use all of the animal.

☐ and they only ate the heart.

☐ and they showed off the furs they got.

3. The Iroquoian tribes were known as a

☐ good group of nomads.

☐ warriors who fought to get land.

☐ the extinct tribes from Newfoundland.

☐ farming group.

4. They had **raiding** parties in spring and fall. **Raiding** means:

☐ trading

☐ buying

☐ looting

☐ celebration

5. Pemmican was a mixture of:

☐ corn, squash and beans.

☐ pelican meat and salt.

☐ dried and powered meat, melted fat and berries.

☐ fur and spruce gum for sealing teepees.

6. The Plains First Nations lived:

☐ on the Plain in Spain.

☐ in a diverse and sometimes difficult environment.

☐ in the middle of the forest.

☐ all over Canada.

7. The process of tanning hide was:

☐ easy and done quickly.

☐ done by the men in the tribe.

☐ a long and difficult one.

☐ only done on buffalo hide.

8. The totem pole is a depiction of the symbols

☐ belonging to the ancestry of the tribe.

☐ of the weather the tribe hoped to have

☐ the animals the tribe ate.

☐ all the children in the village.

9. The Slave and the Chipewayan believed the soul took a special journey after death. The soul crossed a lake in a

☐ flying canoe

☐ birch bark canoe.

☐ stone canoe.

☐ the chief's canoe.

Self- Evaluation: What I did in the unit. Name Name _____

The best part of the unit was……

_____

_____

_____

I learned about……..

_____

_____

_____

I want to learn more about….

_____

_____

_____

My Work Habits:

	Yes	Sometimes	I need to try harder.
I listened to instructions.			
I worked independently.			
I completed my work on time and with care.			
I added supporting details to my work.			
I was a good group member			

Student Assessment Rubric

	Level One	Level Two	Level Three	Level Four
B A S I C C O N C E P T S	• Shows little understanding of concepts. • Rarely gives complete explanations. • Teacher support is intensive.	• Shows some understanding of concepts. • Gives appropriate, but incomplete explanations. • Some teacher assistance is needed.	• Shows understanding of most concepts. • Usually gives complete or nearly complete explanations. • Infrequent teacher support is needed.	• Shows understanding of all or almost all concepts • Consistently gives appropriate and complete explanations independently. • No teacher support is needed.
C O M M U N I C A T I O N	• Rarely communicates with clarity and precision in written and oral work • Rarely uses appropriate terminology and vocabulary • Intensive teacher prompts needed to use correct vocabulary	• Sometimes communicates with clarity and precision in written and oral work • Rarely uses appropriate terminology and vocabulary • Occasional teacher prompts needed to use correct vocabulary	• Usually communicates with clarity and precision in written and oral work • Usually uses appropriate terminology and vocabulary • Infrequent teacher prompts needed to use correct vocabulary	• Consistently communicates with clarity and precision in written and oral work with supporting details • Consistently uses appropriate terminology and vocabulary • No teacher prompts needed to use correct vocabulary
C O N C E P T A P P L I C A T I O N	• Student displays little understanding of how concepts are connected • Rarely applies concepts and skills in a variety of contexts • Intensive teacher support is needed to encourage application of concepts	• Student sometimes displays understanding of how concepts are connected • Sometimes applies concepts and skills in a variety of contexts • Occasional teacher support is needed to encourage application of concepts	• Student usually displays understanding of how concepts are connected • Usually applies concepts and skills in a variety of contexts • Infrequent teacher support is needed to encourage application of concepts	• Student consistently displays understanding of how concepts are connected • Almost always applies concepts and skills in a variety of contexts • No teacher support is needed to encourage application of concepts

More Brainwork!

- Create your own word search for each of the First Nations.

- Create a diorama of a First Nation's village using found materials. Make sure you include written information and labels to describe your diorama.

- Research and report on important contributions that Aboriginal Peoples have made to Canada.

- Research and report on how the environment affected one of the First Nations.

- Investigate a creation story and write your own version.

- Create a class website that celebrates Canada's Aboriginals contributions. Examples of class projects, artwork, dioramas, other Internet links and research reports may be included.

Great Work!

Keep up the effort!

Keep up the effort!

_____

Quality work!